DJ

Printed in the United Kingdom by
MPG Books Ltd, Bodmin

Published by SMT, an imprint of
Sanctuary Publishing Limited
Sanctuary House
45–53 Sinclair Road
London W14 0NS
United Kingdom

www.sanctuarypublishing.com

Picture Credits: Rex Features,
and Daniel Newman
Design and Editorial: Essential Works

ISBN: 1-84492-038-0

XTREME

DJ

Tom Frederikse

smt

CONTENTS

INTRODUCTION

Welcome to *Xtreme DJ*, the best and quickest way to learn
the basics of DJing.

Since about 1990, DJs have become the most important
part of the music world. DJs choose the music that we all
listen to. DJs produce the biggest hit records in the world.
DJs are the performers that people watch when they go
out at weekends. DJs even make the records themselves
– the actual artists – that fill the charts. So at long last, DJs
are being recognised as proper musicians that play the newest
musical instrument: the turntable, the record deck, the 'wheels
of steel'. Finally, we've come out of the booth and onto the
stage. The age of the DJ has arrived.

DJing is a new art that is still developing and evolving, but
the basic foundations are inside these pages. This book will
teach you how to get started, how to use the gear, how to
do some impressive tricks, how to scratch and how to make a
record of your own performance. After you finish the book, you
can use it to combine the elements in your own way and add
your own twists to create an individual style that pleases you.
After all, doing it your own way, in your own time, is what
music is really all about.

Learning music and DJing has to be fun – or no one would do it
– and this book is designed to be enjoyed and for having fun.

Now let's meet DJ Scratch, your guide to the rest of the book...

MEET YOUR TUTOR

DJ Scratch is a legend. He grew up in Manchester, England, listening to his brother's records on his dad's stereo. Using old vintage '80s decks (inherited from Dad) and a second-hand mixer bought from the back of a magazine, he locked himself into his bedroom and emerged six months later a highly-skilled DJ. He played a few friends' parties, started hanging around the DJ booth in the local club and made friends with a resident DJ who (after constant badgering) relented and gave him a slot of his own on a slow night. Everyone was amazed by Scratch's smooth and innovative mixing, and the rest is history. Scratch now travels the world as one of the biggest-ever superstar DJs.

SCRATCH IS HERE TO GUIDE YOU...

The lessons are short and to the point. Each one starts with a clearly-stated goal so that you know what you're supposed to learn and where you're headed. The theory sections are made as simple as possible and are followed by exercises to demonstrate the goal and suggested moves for you to practise.

TEST YOU...

The lessons end with a summary test so that you can see how you're doing. Some are harder than others, so don't expect to ace every test first time. Remember: DJ Scratch didn't get to be a superstar DJ by not practising.

ADVISE YOU...

There's plenty of advice for you in this book, including tips to make you a better DJ, to help you find and choose tunes and even how to get gigs. It's not an easy road to superstar DJ heaven, but these should at least show you a couple of short cuts.

MAKE YOU LAUGH...

'If you don't enjoy it, don't do it.' That's the motto that Scratch lives by. You have to laugh at so many things in life – most professional DJs in the music business would have dropped out by now if they couldn't have laughed at some of the worst things that happened along the way. When your skills completely desert you, making the set sound terrible or when the promoter gets the dates wrong and you travel all day for nothing or when the airline loses your record box – what else can you do?

DJ EQUIPMENT

If you don't already have any DJ equipment at all, then Scratch suggests you read, at least Lesson 1, before you buy anything. It'll teach you the basics of the gear and might help you know what to look for when forking out your money. If you already do have gear – and probably most of you do – then don't worry. Just get stuck in and you'll soon learn how to use what you've got in the best ways possible.

HEADPHONES You can use any headphones in the world for DJing (and you probably will), but always remember that they won't last long – so don't spend too much on them.

SLIPMATS A slipmat is just a piece of felt material that sits on the platter of the deck underneath the record, allowing you to stop or spin the record on top of it. The only thing that matters is that it slips a lot.

MIXERS A mixer has two functions: it boosts the very weak signal that comes out of the deck to a higher level, which is needed for power amplifiers, and it allows the DJ to choose, mix and balance the turntables (and CD players, etc) and monitor them on headphones.

TURNTABLES Basically, the 'deck' plays records by dragging a tiny piece of diamond (the 'needle') through the grooves and sending the sound down the wires towards the mixer. The deck's got a tone arm, which holds a cartridge at its end. There's also a switch to choose between 33 rpm and 45 rpm, and another control that adjusts the speed more finely called the 'pitch shift', 'pitch control' or 'vari-speed'.

CARTRIDGES The expensive cartridges do tend to last longer and skip a bit less, but they rarely sound any better. So long as you set up the tone arm properly, you'll be just as happy with a cheaper version.

LESSONS

CONNECTIONS AND SET-UP

Even if you know your deck from your mixer, you're lost if you don't know how to plug it up. Plus, you have to set up just a couple of things before you're ready to roll. So, let's get started…

YOUR GOALS

GOAL 1
To understand how the bits connect up to each other.

GOAL 2
To properly set the weighting of your tone arm.

THEORY

So, what goes where and how do you set it up? Start by memorising this rule: 'Ins connect to Outs!' The basic DJ set-up is really simple and quick to plug up. Then the only really crucial thing you need to do is to set the right weight on your tone arm.

IN PRACTICE

To get the sound from DJ to dance floor, let's go step by step...

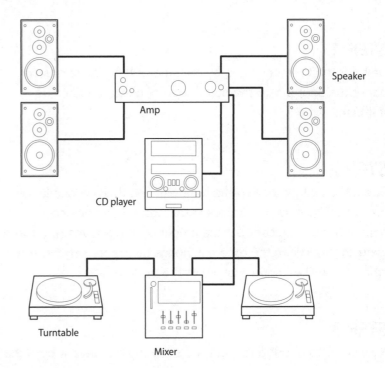

STEP 1

Each turntable has a stereo audio lead coming out of it that gets connected to the PHONO inputs of a channel on the back of the mixer. There is also a ground (or 'earth') wire that gets connected to the earth point (usually a screw on the back of each channel) to avoid feedback. CD players don't have earth leads so they just get plugged into the LINE inputs instead of the PHONO inputs on the back of mixers.

STEP 2

The mixer must now be connected to the amp. Take a stereo audio lead and plug the main outputs (left and right for stereo) of the mixer into the main inputs of the power amp.

STEP 3

Usually you'll just plug the headphones straight into the jack input on the mixer.

STEP 4

Finally, connect the amp to the speakers.

IN PRACTICE

PART 2

To set-up the proper weighting on your tone arm…

STEP 1

First, let the tone arm hang by the side of the platter at just about the spot where the outer edge of a record would be if it were there.

STEP 2

Screw the weight well up the tone arm and then gradually take weight off by screwing it back in the other direction until the needle hangs at just about the height of the grooves (if a record were there). When the tone arm hangs balanced, set the free-spinning number-marked wheel at the back to '0'.

STEP 3

Now set it to about two grams by screwing the weight back the other way (as much as recommended in the manufacturer's manual) – and then a tiny bit more so that you have a bit of help while learning to DJ. Be careful, however, not to put too much on or you'll wear out your records quickly and they'll become crackly.

TIP

A great way to cheat when you don't have time to set up the weight properly is to tape a penny or two on top of the cartridge. Of course, this could damage your records quite quickly if you go over the top, so, if possible, set it up properly.

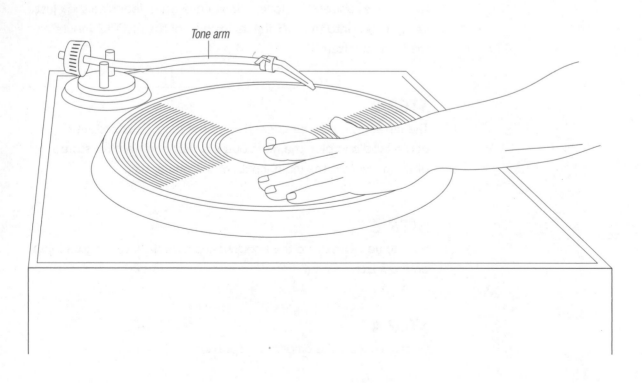

Tone arm

EXERCISE

1. Try setting up the weight as you've just learned to do, then experiment by adding more and then less weight and see how far you need to go to make the needle fall flat on the record or jump up and down. This way you'll really know what 'too much' and 'too little' weight is.

PROBLEM?

If you hear a low drone or buzz through the system, it probably means that you haven't connected the earth lead on one of the decks. As soon as you connect the earth, the noise should stop.

TEST

QUESTION 1
Name the main bits in a basic DJ set-up?

QUESTION 2
What does the earth lead get connected to?

QUESTION 3
What's the most important thing to set up on a turntable?

BEATS, BARS AND CUEING UP

It's impossible to know where you are on a record – or where to mix in and out – if you don't understand the very basics of music: beats and bars. Once you understand that, you gotta get jiggy with it, by putting your hand all over the grooves. So be ready to get touchy feely!

YOUR GOALS

GOAL 1
To understand beats and bars.

GOAL 2
To cue up a record to a certain spot.

THEORY

Beats are the building blocks of music. The rhythm – the constant push – of every song is made up of evenly spaced pulses called 'beats'. Beats never stop running and they do not depend on whether or not the drums are playing. Even a song without any drums at all will still have the same pulse made of the same beats as every other song.

Beats are most easily spotted in good old plodding house or garage tunes. Check the first tune on the CD, where the bass drum thuds once for each beat of the bar – this is the easily-recognised '1, 2, 3, 4' that dominates this style of music.

In all dance music, beats are organised into groups of four with each group of four called a 'bar'. Within each bar, the four beats have a regularly-occurring pattern in which the first and third beats are stronger, downward pulses called 'down' or 'on' beats. The second and fourth beats are the secondary, upward pulses called 'up' or 'off' beats.

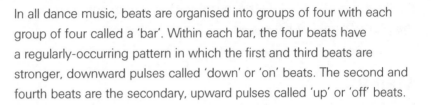

TRACK 1 CD

IN PRACTICE

STEP 1

Now, let's get used to touching the vinyl. Start by putting a record on the deck, and set it spinning. Using a couple of right fingers, 'grab' the record in the middle of the grooves (on the opposite side of the vinyl to the tone arm) by pressing down on the vinyl. If you press hard enough, the record will stop spinning and will 'float' on the slipmat, while the platter underneath continues to spin at full speed. While holding the vinyl, slowly move it a few inches forwards and backwards, and then hold it still again. Then finally let go of it with a little 'push' so that it very quickly rides the platter again at full speed.

STEP 2

Now let's 'cue' the record up to the first sound of the first tune. When the music begins to play, grab the record by stopping it physically with your hand just after you hear the first beat. While holding the record in place with your hand on the grooves, try a 'rewind' by moving your hand onto the label of the record (quickly so as not to lose your place and with only one hand so that the other is free to work the mixer).

STEP 3

With your first or second finger, wind the record anti-clockwise. As you wind it backwards, you'll hear the tune play in reverse but keep going until you have passed the first beat (until you hear silence). Now move your hand back onto the grooves (quickly again so as not to let the record move more than a half-inch or so).

STEP 4

Now that you've found the first beat, make sure of this by slowly moving the vinyl forward a bit under the needle. When you hear the beginning of the sound, move it quickly backwards again to the silence before the first beat (then forwards and backwards again many times to 'see' where the sound starts). Remember to keep your eyes on the label of the record to find a reference point to know where the first beat is physically on the record. Now let go of the record so that it plays at the correct speed right from the first beat by keeping your hand relaxed and trying to feel the pull of the motor as you pull it over that first beat.

PROBLEM?

Make sure you don't press down too much or the platter will stop. If the record and the platter stop together when you're handling the record, then you're pressing it too hard – so, lighten up just a little!

EXERCISE

1. Choose an easy record to try this with (something not too fast and, ideally, a house or garage record). Try making the 'wukka-wukka' sound until you're comfortable with it. Then try cueing it up from the beginning.

TIP

The snare drum in most tunes plays on the second and fourth beat of every bar, and this is a good way of checking yourself and making sure that you're counting properly.

TEST

QUESTION 1
What is the difference between a 'note' of a song and a 'beat' of music?

QUESTION 2
How many beats are in a bar?

QUESTION 3
What is an 'off-beat'?

DROP MIXING

The first and easiest kind of mixing is called drop mixing, because that's all it is – you drop the needle just about anywhere and mix from there. The new record is faded into the mix while the old one fades out. You don't need to worry too much about making the two records match (though it would make it sound a bit better if you did), just try to always do it smoothly.

THEORY

Drop mixing is the art of bringing a new record into the mix and getting rid of the old one without a gap between them. With a record already playing on one deck, the first thing you need to do is to find the point on the second record from which you want to start mixing it in over the first.

IN PRACTICE

STEP 1

Put a record on the first deck (the left one) and set it playing. Choose a spot in it that you think would be a good place to fade it out (the 'mix-out' spot). Then put another record on the second deck, and choose a place that might be good to 'mix in' from (just choose the beginning for now).

STEP 2

Start by listening only to the new track in the headphones (by pressing the 'PFL' or 'solo button' on that channel). Let the record play just past the chosen 'in' point, and then quickly grab it and wind it back (with the needle still on the record, of course) about one full turn further than that first beat at the beginning. This gives you time to reposition your hand in a comfortable position.

STEP 3

Hold the record steady and, when you are ready to drop mix and the first record gets just about to its mix-out point, release the record and at the same time with your other hand, bring the crossfader (see p21) over from the left side to the right. Try to do both actions on the first beat of the bar in each tune so that the two records seem to blend together in time and rhythm.

YOUR GOAL

To mix from one record to the next by drop mixing.

TIP
Whenever you're listening to a record and trying to find cue points (or 'in' and 'out' points), always count '1, 2, 3, 4' at all times so that you know where the beats and bars are. It makes it easier to match up the tunes if you're thinking in terms of matching up the beats and bars.

PROBLEM?

If you hit the 'PFL' or 'Solo' button on a channel and still hear nothing, it's probably because there's no record playing on that channel – or because that channel's actually turned off or the phono/line switch is set to 'line' instead of 'phono'.

EXERCISE

1. Its time to do your first drop mix! Choose two records (ideally both featuring long sections of drums), and listen through them to choose your in and out points. Set one playing and try drop mixing the other one at the end of a section of drums. Don't forget to keep both channel faders up about three-quarters of the way at all times, and to do the switch over on the crossfader only.

TEST

QUESTION 1
What is the 'PFL' or 'Solo' button?

QUESTION 2
What does the crossfader do?

QUESTION 3
What is a cue point?

BEAT MIXING 1

Now it's time to get a bit more serious. Beat mixing is the heart and soul of DJing 'cos it makes your mixes sound groovy and danceable. When you beat mix two records together, the audience should hear no separation of sound between them and, if you're very good at it, they shouldn't even be able to tell that a new record has started. It takes a long time to get great at it, but not very long to get good enough to impress yourself!

YOUR GOALS

GOAL 1
To understand tempo and phrasing.

GOAL 2
To understand the basics of beat mixing.

GOAL 3
To beat mix by hand.

THEORY

Beat matching is when a DJ plays two records at the same time and both running from the beginning of a musical phrase, having adjusted the speed of one of them so that they run at the same speed and tempo ('in sync'). This allows the DJ to then beat mix the two records (for a few bars usually) when mixing from one to the other. In order for beat mixing not to sound like a car crash, the two records must keep perfect time and their sounds, beats and music must all blend together.

The speed that the turntable spins at is just called the 'speed', and it is measured in revolutions per minute (or rpm), as in 33 rpm and 45 rpm. The speed of a song, however, is always called the 'tempo', and it is measured in beats per minute (or bpm). You can only change the tempo of a tune by changing the speed of the deck.

We have already seen that the beats of a tune are organised into bars of four beats each, but there is another group which is larger, called a 'phrase', which consists usually of 8 or 16 bars. Beat mixing depends on spotting the beginnings of phrases accurately, because it is necessary to match the phrases of two records perfectly in order for them to sound good when they are playing together at the same time.

There are two ways to beat mix: by hand and by using the pitch control. Both methods, however, are basically just clever ways to keep two records running at the same speed. Speed is the key thing here. Even if you try to beat mix two copies of the same record, they will still probably run at slightly different speeds after a while (because no machine is perfect). You'll still have to use your beat-mixing skill to make them run at the exact same speed in order to stay in sync.

Making two records run at the same speed is a bit like two trains trying to drive together down the tracks side-by-side. No matter how hard the drivers try to drive at the same speed, sooner or later one train will go a tiny bit faster or slower than the other.

The first trick is figure out which one is speeding up or slowing down. Think of sitting in a train while looking out the window and seeing another train go slowly past the window. Sometimes, it's hard to tell which one is going faster or slower, and it's impossible to bring both trains even (by speeding up or slowing down) until you know which one is doing what.

Beat mixing two records is almost the same problem. You need to start by deciding which record is ahead or behind – going too fast or too slow – and then you need to correct that problem by doing the opposite thing to it until the problem is fixed. And you have to keep doing this (the whole time) while the two records are running together.

IN PRACTICE

STEP 1

To begin your first beat mix, use two records of similar tempo (such as CD Tracks 3 and 9), and make sure both pitch controls are at '0'. Cue both tunes up to where the drums start, set them running together at the same time (or start with a good drop mix so that both records start in sync at the right time) and then you can think about which one is pulling ahead or falling behind. The quicker they fall out of time, the bigger the difference in tempo between the two records and the more you'll have to adjust the speed of one of them.

STEP 2

If you need to, slow down the record... Let your finger or thumb brush against the side of that record platter for an instant. The more pressure you apply, or the longer that you apply it for, the more it will slow down. Another method is to squeeze the spindle at the centre of the turntable for just a short moment. This will slow it down, but has a more subtle effect.

If you need to speed up the record... put your finger on the label of the record and push downwards into the platter to disable the slipmat. Then move the record onwards slightly faster in a clockwise direction. For smaller adjustments, turn the spindle faster or physically push the record onwards clockwise (but not the platter itself!).

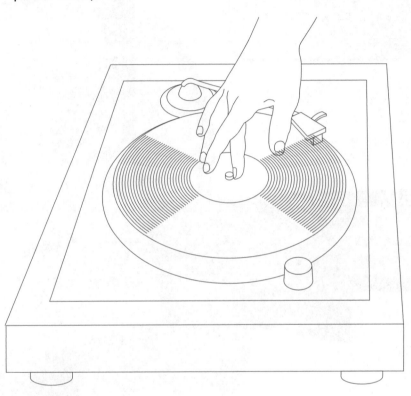

STEP 3

Once you've managed to bring the two into sync for an instant, you'll probably notice that they fall out again rather quickly. Try to guess which record is going faster or slower again and make a small adjustment on the pitch control in the opposite way (for example, if record two is going too fast, pull down its pitch control a little bit). Now decide which record is doing what, and repeat the whole thing again. By doing this over and over again you will continue to make the problem smaller and smaller – and eventually unnoticeable.

STEP 4

While you're practising, leave the crossfader mostly in the middle to hear both records in the speaker, but, to simulate a real performance, start your beat mixing with only the first record in the speakers and the second record only in the headphones. When you finally get both records running at the same speed, throw the crossfader to the middle so that the crowd can hear both.

TIP
Every tune is organised into phrases (but not always of the same length), and the beginnings of phrases are often marked by a cymbal crash at the beginning and by a drum fill at the end.

PROBLEM?

If you can't figure out which tune is going faster or slower, just try speeding or slowing either one of them. The problem will then get bigger, and it becomes easier to tell what's going on.

EXERCISE

1. Using two records that are quite close in tempo (or even better, two copies of the same record) start by drop mixing them. Decide which is going too fast or slow and do the moves to fix it. If it all goes wrong (which it will!) just stop and start again with a drop mix.

TEST

QUESTION 1
What is the difference between speed and tempo?

QUESTION 2
What is a phrase of music?

QUESTION 3
What is beat mixing?

QUESTION 4
Can you name two ways to beat mix by hand?

BEAT MIXING 2

Now it's time to use the other bits on the decks that we haven't looked at yet: the pitch controls. This requires a bit of fancy finger work and a lot of practice, but once you master these goals, you'll be ready to perform a whole set in one go (and make it sound good!).

YOUR GOALS

GOAL 1
To beat mix with the pitch control.

GOAL 2
To finish the beat mix.

THEORY

Once you get the hang of beat mixing with two records that are very close in tempo you'll be ready to try it all over again with records of quite different tempos. For this you need to use the pitch control, which will speed up or slow down a tune by up to (usually) 8 per cent, but remember that, as the tempo (and speed) increases or decreases, so does the pitch. So a track played at a speed much faster than normal will go all 'Mickey Mouse', or if played too slowly will sound lazy and slurred.

IN PRACTICE

STEP 1

Start by drop-mixing two records from the beginnings of similar-sounding phrases (or at least phrases with similar drum patterns). Decide whether the second track is going faster or slower: are the beats racing ahead so that you reach the end of a phrase too soon? Or are they dragging so that it falls behind? Try listening to similar instruments in the two tunes together to compare them – the bass drums of each track or maybe the high hats or snares.

STEP 2

When you've decided what the problem is, use the pitch control to make it go faster or slower. You'll have to use the pitch control quite vigorously to imitate the movements that you were doing by hand in the last lesson. You might need to over-compensate for a record going too slowly by jerking the pitch control up quite high for just a moment and then yanking it back down. Remember that if one record is at a faster tempo than the other, the pitch control will have to stay lower than '0' for most of the beat mix – as well as having to pull the control even lower to bring it into sync before returning the control to its not-quite-so-low position, for the two to run together.

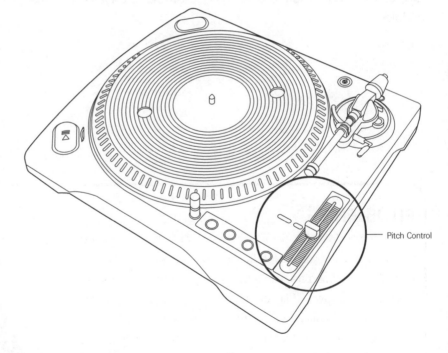

Pitch Control

LISTEN TO CD TRACK 4: An example of a tune with a big bass line, plenty of instrumentation and loads of vocals. If you were to beat mix another tune over this, it would have to be very 'empty' (without a bass line or vocals).

STEP 3

MIXING OUT

Once you manage to get your tempos to match up, remember that you must also make the phrases of the two records move from one to the other naturally, and this usually means that you can't do a beat mix of less than eight bars. When you bring a new record into the mix, do it at the beginning of a phrase while bringing the crossfader to the centre on the first beat. Likewise, you need to fade out of the mix so that you fall into the new tune on the first beat of a phrase.

STEP 4

MATCHING LEVELS

It is crucial that both tunes are at the same volume so that there is no noticeable change in the overall volume when mixing two tunes (never bring in a track louder than the last). The crossfader is designed to keep the overall level constant, so the level often drops a tiny bit when you move away from the edges on the hard left or hard right – this is in order to make up for the fact there is only one record in the mix at those points, rather than the two records that share the mix when the crossfader is anywhere in the middle.

TIP

Don't try to mix two records that both have vocals or big bass lines running, as it tends to sound messy. Mixing two tunes of very different tempos is also very difficult to do without one or the other sounding obviously too fast or slow.

PROBLEM?

If your mixer doesn't have a crossfader, you'll need to mix by adjusting the volumes using the channel faders. When you bring in the second track in a beat mix, introduce it at about three-quarters level while leaving the first track at full volume. As you start to switch over to the second track, any rise in the second track must be matched by a drop in the first one. Never bring both faders to the top at the same time, as you'll then have the full force of both records – and the mix would be very, very loud!

EXERCISE

1. To equal out the volumes, listen to a record on each turntable – without beat-mixing them – and see which one sounds louder when the channel fader is at the same height. When you notice a louder one you'll know this channel fader must always be set a bit lower for that record (you could even make a note of this on the outer sleeve).

2. With the crossfader all the way over to one side, beat match the record on the other deck (in the headphones only!). When they are matched, cue the second tune up and set it running from a spot 8 or 16 bars before the point where you want to beat mix the two. Just as that spot comes, throw the crossfader over and listen to how they sound together. If it sounds good, keep them both in for a while. If not, move the crossfader quickly.

TEST

QUESTION 1
What is the maximum that a pitch control can usually increase the speed of the deck?

QUESTION 2
What is the disadvantage of using the pitch control at its maximum or minimum?

QUESTION 3
Why is matching levels so important?

QUESTION 4
How can you use the channel faders in place of a crossfader?

QUESTION 5
Which particular sounds tend not to blend well if beat-mixed together?

EASY TRICKS

This is where you start to add a bit of sparkle to your mixing. After you can drop mix and beat mix well enough to keep a smooth sound going in your mix non-stop for 30 minutes, then it's time to spice it up by throwing in the odd trick.

THEORY

You'll probably recognise the sound of the 'switch' and 'fill' tricks as soon as you do them. You know that old cliché where the DJ goes 'REWIND!'? Well, that actually is the trick known as 'spinback'. All three of these tricks can be thrown in while you're doing your normal set. They don't interrupt the flow of the mix at all – rather these tricks make your mix sound better and make it more exciting. They can be done one at a time every few minutes, or one right after the other. Just remember: don't do too many too often (less is more, man!).

YOUR GOALS

GOAL 1
To perform switch tricks.

GOAL 2
To perform fill tricks.

GOAL 3
To perform a spinback.

IN PRACTICE

SWITCH TRICK

The line/phono switch, at the top of each channel on the mixer, controls whether that channel will listen to its phono input or its line input on the back of the mixer. Usually, if you are DJing with vinyl, there will be nothing plugged into the line input on the back (because the two decks are plugged into the two phono inputs), so when you change the switch to 'line', you hear nothing and the switch effectively cuts out the sound. This allows you to make rhythms with the tune plugged into that channel by toggling the line/phono switch quickly and rhythmically. Switch tricks can be especially cool when done on a vocals- or music-only section (it makes it sound like a 'gated' or 'transformer' effect).

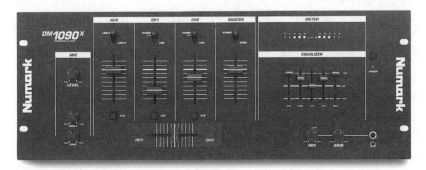

A mixer

LISTEN TO CD TRACK 3: The vocals in this track demonstrate the 'gated' or 'transformer' effect.

FILL TRICKS

In this trick, you swap to the record you are about to mix just for the last bar of a phrase before returning quickly back to the first tune, using the crossfader. With this technique, you can use the new record to create a kind of 'drum fill' to set up the next phrase of the original record. Of course you could do this at several points throughout a phrase as well, and it works really brilliantly (if both phrases happen to work together musically and rhythmically). If you're really keen, you can even create new drum patterns by switching between two different beat-mixed tunes quite often within a phrase or even within a single bar.

SPINBACKS

On the last beat of a phrase, just when you would probably be coming out of the mix, suddenly grab the grooves of the first record and spin it sharply backwards – then quickly crossfade to the new tune on the first beat of the next phrase. Of course, some tunes work better than others for this trick and you'll just have to keep searching for the perfect one. An even more dramatic version of the spinback is (instead of spinning it backwards) to turn the power off (yes, really!) and just let the record grind to a halt. Crossfade over to the new tune on the beat where it would have hit anyway – and keep the overall groove going for the dancers!

EXERCISE

1. Here's an easy, but brilliant, version of the switch trick for you to try. Toggle the switch so that it is in the phono position only when the actual bass drum notes play. That is, turn it on briefly for each beat of the bar, and turn it off immediately after the bass drum hits, so that there is a short silence between each bass drum (a total of four on/offs in each bar). You can also perform this trick using the channel fader by throwing it up and back down again very quickly, but this is very difficult and will never be as quick as the switch method.

PROBLEM?

If you find that a record won't spinback easily, it may be because the middle hole is too tight – if so, carefully enlarge it a bit with a pair of scissors. Also, if a record is warped at all, a spinback will usually throw the needle off.

TIP

The special switch trick in this exercise takes a quick hand. Some people find it easier to use the thumb as a spring to tap out the rhythm against the pressure of a finger that holds the switch in the off position.

TEST

QUESTION 1
What is the line/phono switch?

QUESTION 2
What is the effect called 'gating' or 'transformer'?

QUESTION 3
What is the fill trick?

QUESTION 4
What is a spinback?

ADVANCED TRICKS

Once you get the hang of the easier tricks in the last lesson, it's
time to move on up a class. Here you'll learn a couple of moves
that should impress even the best DJs. They're not easy, but
then, the best things never are, are they?

YOUR GOALS

GOAL 1
To perform phasing and
back-to-back mixing.

GOAL 2
To perform a cappella
mixing.

THEORY

Here are three tricks that are quite different from each other. Phasing is a trick that requires two copies of the same record, but it's really worth it, 'cos it's really cool. Back-to-back mixing is really just a natural extension of beat mixing. An 'a cappella' is a mix on a record that has a vocal track with no music or drums at all – just the solo voice. Many 12" singles will feature an a cappella mix as the last track on side B. Use your imagination and try to think of every vocal you've ever heard (or, at least, quite a few) to find a combination to mix with instrumental tunes.

IN PRACTICE

PHASING

Start by beat mixing the two copies of the record at exactly the same passage so that they mirror each other. Get the two records as tight in time as you can and then throw the crossfader into the middle so that you can hear both records in equal volume. You should already notice that the sound of the two records together has a strange metallic or alien quality. Try nudging one of the two records just enough to throw it just ever so slightly out of time and you should notice the effect gets wider. When you then correct the timing problem you should notice the phasing effect become tighter again. You may occasionally manage to get the two records so tightly beat-matched that the sound seems to disappear almost entirely. If so, well done – that's a perfect phase.

LISTEN TO CD TRACK 7: Halfway through this tune is a demonstration of what the phasing effect sounds like.

BACK-TO-BACK MIXING

Use your two copies of the same record and, once you have beat mixed them both on the two decks, nudge one of them enough so that it falls exactly one half of a beat behind the other. You should be hearing the bass drums of one record playing in the spaces between the bass drums of the other, resulting in eight bass drums in each bar (counting all the bass drums in both records). This isn't easy and sometimes it takes a few attempts until you nudge it just the right amount. Having kept the crossfader hard to one side while cueing up and nudging, you can now let the two records play (one half beat apart) and throw the crossfader over swiftly (and then swiftly back again) in order to add an extra bass drum from the second record into the mix (in-between two bass drums of the other record).

A CAPPELLA MIXING

This one is simply playing the vocal-only record over the top of the instrument-only record and listening to see if they sound good together. Mixing an a cappella vocal over another tune is just like doing a beat mix, except that it's harder to find an instrumental record and an a cappella record that go well together. Also, remember that most a cappella vocals don't start on the first beat of the bar, so it can be difficult to figure out the groove of the vocal in order to beat mix it properly in time over the other track. In general, mixing an a cappella is not an easy task, and even the best of us will only get it close and never exactly right! But that's okay because a singer's timing is never perfect anyway so you have an automatic bit of leeway in which to mess up. (Still, though, try to be aware of the singer's groove and make it fit the track as best as you can.)

LISTEN TO CD TRACKS 9 AND 10: Hear examples of vocals-only and instruments-only tracks.

CD TRACK 9

CD TRACK 10

TIP

If you have to change the speed of an a cappella during the mix, try to use only the pitch control to do it and then use it only in the gaps between vocals where the a cappella is silent (so that no one can hear the record change speed during a vocal note!).

PROBLEM?

If you tend to lose the beat when trying to back-to-back mix, just try to remember to always return the crossfader back to the original side after adding a bass drum so as not to confuse the '1, 2, 3, 4' of the rhythm!

EXERCISE

1. Try back-to-back mixing by beat mixing two copies of the same record and try nudging one to being half a beat behind the other. Listen for the eight bass drums per bar. Practise throwing the crossfader quickly from side to side until you can do a full back-and-forth throw smoothly within the space of one beat.

2. When you do find a potential combination of records for a cappella mixing – or if you don't, use the a cappella (vocal only) and the instrumental of the same track, such as on the Xtreme CD – start by trying to beat-match the two records over and over until you discover a good enough cue point to mix in. Practise making your speed corrections and adjustments to the a cappella record only during the gaps in the vocal so that you cannot hear the speed changes in the singing.

TEST

QUESTION 1
What is phasing?

QUESTION 2
What is back-to-back mixing?

QUESTION 3
What is an a cappella?

SCRATCHING

Scratching is the most well-known DJ trademark. Everybody immediately recognises that distinctive sound as soon as they hear it, and they know that the DJ is getting hot and that the music is about to get exciting. On the other hand, scratching is the hardest part of DJing to learn, because you have to develop a completely new skill and dexterity. However, there are a couple of easy scratches that can be learned quite quickly and that should make you sound awesome straight away!

YOUR GOALS

GOAL 1
To perform the baby scratch.

GOAL 2
To perform the forward and backward scratches.

GOAL 3
To perform a scribble.

GOAL 4
To perform a chop.

THEORY

Before we start, make sure that your slipmat is very slippy – if not, you'll never scratch right! The baby scratch is the most basic of scratches and is the basis for all other scratches. It's sometimes called the 'classic wukka-wukka' because that's what it sounds like. The idea is to move the record back and forth under the needle to the beat of another record. The other scratches build on the baby, so make sure you're comfortable with each one before you move on.

IN PRACTICE

BABY

Start with just one record on one deck and cue the needle up to a big drum sound somewhere near the outer edge of the vinyl. Using the same hand technique as you used for cueing and mixing, simply move the record sharply (or slowly, at first) back and forth so that the one drum beat (or whatever sound) can be heard going forwards then backwards. The faster you pull and push the record, the shorter and higher the scratch sound.

LISTEN TO CD TRACK 6: This has useful sounds for scratching, including drums and percussion, as well as vocal bits.

FORWARD AND BACKWARD

The forward scratch is a combination of a baby scratch and some crossfader moves to chop up (or 'edit') the scratched sound. By using the fader at the right moment, you can get rid of only a part of a chosen scratched sound and leave the rest. For example, a bass drum, when scratched slowly, makes a sound like 'cha ka' and, using a forward technique, you could kill the second part of the sound by throwing the fader over immediately after the first bit of the sound (thereby leaving only the sound of 'cha', without the 'ka' after it. This is often done to the rhythm of a track playing on the first deck by keeping the crossfader over to the left and only throwing it to the middle for the short blast of the 'cha' sound from the forward scratch on deck two. The crossfader is then thrown all the way back to the left while you pull the scratch record back and set it up for another forward. Keep repeating it as long you can make it sound rhythmic and groovy.

In a nutshell, the forward scratch is: open crossfader, forward pull, close crossfader, return record to original position, repeat. For the backward scratch, keep the crossfader technique the same but reverse the scratch moves so that you start with the backwards move, and return it again by moving forward.

SCRIBBLE

Do your baby moves with a short break in-between each scratch and then tense and shake your arm quickly but in a small movement so that it looks like your arm is freaking out. The sound should also sound like a bit of a freaked-out scratch where the music shimmers.

CHOP

This one is based on the forward. You need some serious crossfader technique to do the chop because the moves are quick. Practise sliding the crossfader quickly back and forth by flicking it with your finger and thumb in time to music, and remember that you need to do this without looking because you always should be watching the vinyl to remember the spot where you need to return to for the next scratch. The idea of the chop is to chop (or edit) out part of a forward scratch so that only part of a sound is heard. The classic chop is to use only the beginning or middle of a very recognisable word or sound so that the audience hears enough of the sound to full monty.

TIP

The forward scratch is especially cool when you scratch a vocal word. Practise scratching the vocal word at an even speed so that the word is clearly heard and understandable when repeated over and over. Then practise closing the crossfader before pulling the vinyl back so that the audience doesn't hear it backwards when you're pulling it back. When you do any of these scratches, you can do any rhythm you like – just so long as it's funky!

PROBLEM?

Remember to keep your hand well away from the tone arm while scratching and, if the needle jumps when you scratch, just try it more slowly until you learn better control.

EXERCISE

1. Most sounds on dance records will work well for scratching, but start by trying to scratch percussion and drum sounds, because they are easiest. Practise baby scratching different sounds in time to a slow record, and then try faster records and more complicated rhythms until you start to feel comfortable with the moves and the grooves. Start getting some control over the sound by running another track on the other deck, and do a single scratch in time to it on the first beat of every bar and then (if you're feeling confident) on every beat of the bar.

2. Practise by recording yourself on a cassette tape forward scratching a vocal word over another tune and listen to where the rhythm isn't even or the word isn't understandable or where the scratching isn't even.

TEST

QUESTION 1
What is the most important thing about slipmats when scratching?

QUESTION 2
What is the 'wukka wukka' sound?

QUESTION 3
What sounds are the easiest to scratch and generally sound the best?

QUESTION 4
What is the scribble?

DIGITAL MIXING

Why would you want to mix with CDs? You can't put your hand on a spinning CD and you can't even see the grooves to know where you are. Sure, there are some drawbacks – but there are plenty more advantages as well, and I don't mean just that CDs weigh a lot less than vinyl tunes! The other kind of digital mixing uses computers and tunes stored as MP3 files – but you'll have to download a bit of (free) software to try it out. You never know, you might even prefer digital mixing to vinyl!

THEORY

As you know, using a normal CD player is simple – just connect the leads to a 'line in' on a channel of your mixer – but the special models for DJs (see below) do have a few extra features which are slightly tricky. Most of them offer two methods for cueing up: automatic and manual. In the automatic mode, the player will (all by itself) find a desired song and stop a split-second (or some short amount of time) before the first sound of the track. This method works quite well when you're just listening to CDs, but is less ideal for beat mixing when you need to be in full control of the run-up to the first beat of the tune. Cueing up a CD manually is much more like traditional DJing because it allows you to physically find the exact chosen spot using either a 'jog wheel' (a big rotary control) or a backwards/forwards button.

YOUR GOALS

GOAL 1
To understand the basics of CD mixing.

GOAL 2
To understand and perform CD looping.

GOAL 3
To know the basics of MP3 mixing and technology.

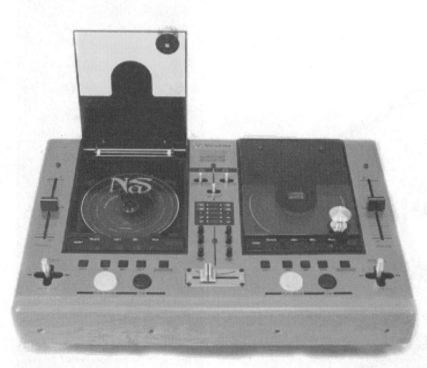

A CD mixer

IN PRACTICE

CDS

If you're cueing up the first beat of a phrase, you'll need to recognise exactly what the 'attack' of a drum note sounds like, because the CD player allows you to approach it so slowly that, at first, you'll only hear the very beginning of the note (the 'attack') before scrolling on to the rest of the sound. It takes a little getting used to, but after cueing CDs a few times you'll soon start to recognise the attack of many different sounds and become adept at cueing just before it. Once you find the exact cue point, most models offer two or four storage buttons that allow you memorise that cue point (by just pressing and holding the 'cue 1' button), and to return to it later (by quickly pressing that same button).

Once you get the CD cued, you'll then need to hit the play button at exactly the right time to throw the CD into play in time with the record that you're beat mixing against. Again, this can take a little practise to learn just how quickly your player reacts and therefore when to hit the button. With CDs rolling on each of the two players, beat matching is done in the traditional way by adjusting the pitch control and then, using the pause and play buttons – or the forward and backward buttons – correcting the position until the tunes are running in sync.

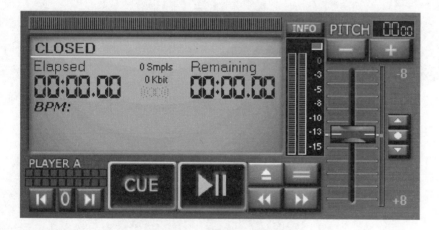

For cueing, all the information you need is displayed on one screen

Because of the nature of CD DJ players that can store cue points, it's easy to extend this to create a 'loop' function. Looping is simply repeating a section of a tune so immediately and so smoothly that it sounds as if the tune itself repeats that way naturally. If your CD player has buttons marked 'loop in' and 'loop out' then you only need set loop points by hitting these at the right time (as the CD is playing) and then hit 'loop' while the CD is playing in the middle of the loop. When the CD reaches the point stored in 'loop out' it will automatically and immediately return to the 'loop in' point and play on until the 'loop out' point – over and over.

MP3s

Probably the two best things about MP3 mixing are not having to lug around record boxes and the wide availability of cheap (and free) MP3 files on the Internet. And, I'm sure you'll agree free stuff is always welcome.

The special feature of MP3 technology is that MP3s are 'compressed' computer files, which means that they are much smaller and take up a lot less memory than normal music files (about one-tenth of a non-MP3 file). This means that you can keep ten times as many tunes on a computer's hard disk or on a CD-ROM.

There are two ways to work with MP3 files. You can either download (or purchase) one of the many all-in-one software packages for computer DJ mixing and do the whole thing on-screen or you can use some software alongside your normal mixer and decks set-up. If you choose the first option then there's not much to say because every computer set-up package is different. They all have some sort of on-screen pictures of little players and usually a 'virtual mixer', but the disadvantage is that you have to do all the work with a mouse or a keypad. A better option would be to use the on-screen package only as a 'player' and plug the audio output of your computer into the line input of a channel of your mixer and think of the computer just as a 'virtual deck' that happens to play MP3s.

Most MP3 mixing software packages offer a few nifty features such as a 'bpm calculator' that tells you the bpm of any file, automatic cue storage and looping functions, and even automatic faders that do smooth fade-ins and fade-outs for you.

When cueing an MP3 file, the first beat of the tune must be located as usual to beat mix it. Just press play until you hear the first sound and then press 'cue', and move the track backwards in slow motion (rewind does this) until you find the top of the sound and then hit 'cue' again. The tune is now cued and ready to play. Load up another tune, cue it the same way and, if possible, enable the computer's 'beat-match' system (the computer will suss the tempos and do the necessary pitch control). You'll notice that MP3 technology has one other amazing feature – the pitch and the speed are separate so that when the speed is made faster or slower, the tune doesn't turn into Mickey Mouse or Darth Vader!

If the system doesn't have automatic beat matching, you'll need to do it the traditional way but using the on-screen pitch control slider, and adjust with the mouse.

EXERCISE

1. Experiment with your CD player by choosing cue points and storing them. When the available memory is full, return to each spot to drop mix the tunes. Practise cueing up and beat matching two CDs – or a CD to a vinyl on one of the decks – to get used to how quickly your player reacts. Choose a few cue points and possible loops, and try to store the points. Return to these points using the buttons to see how accurate your storage technique is. Try to keep a manual loop going for as long as you can without missing a beat.

2. To experiment with MP3s, (if you have a computer set up), try downloading a DJ mixing software package and playing around with it – such as *http://otsdj.com/* or *http://www.mixvibes.com/mv4proeng.htm.*

TEST

QUESTION 1
What are some advantages of mixing CDs?

QUESTION 2
What is the problem with using the auto-cue function on a CD player?

QUESTION 3
What is looping?

QUESTION 4
What is an MP3?

QUESTION 5
What's the big advantage of MP3 files that makes them so popular?

MAKING A DEMO CD

Making a recording of yourself playing a set is just about the best possible way of improving your skills. You'll hear all the mistakes and bad choices of tunes (as well as the good points and the excellent choices!). And anyway, a DJ without a mix tape is like a lawyer without a briefcase – just plain unnatural!

YOUR GOAL

To make a recording of yourself mixing a set.

THEORY

The only way to make a demo mix tape is to record yourself in action. Of course, ideally, you want to record your best-ever set. But, seeing as this is practically impossible, let's settle for the next best thing – a very good set that you can be proud of.

There are two places to record a set – at home alone or in a performance in front of friends or family. Some people really rise to the occasion when performing and need the pressure and excitement of an audience to perform well. Most of us, however, prefer the nice quiet bedroom with a cup of tea, where you can make a million mistakes and start over as many times as you need.

IN PRACTICE

Whatever you use, you only need to connect the master outputs of your mixer to the inputs of the recording machine. The first thing you've got to do is borrow a recording machine (for one or two days only!). There are several options, including: a cassette machine (the loud volume of most dance music means any noise from the tape would not be heard much); a reel-to-reel tape machine (probably better than a cassette machine even if it is more finicky and more hassle); a recordable CD machine (an excellent option if you can find one); or a computer with a digital recording software set-up on a PC or Mac (it's the best quality and you can record many different takes then edit the best bits together afterwards to create one 'perfect' set). Whatever option you choose, the connections will always be the same (remember 'master output to record input') but, as you record, you should always listen to the sound as it comes out of the recording machine rather than from the usual amps/speakers because this will ensure that you hear what is being recorded (and you or a friend can check to see that everything's being recorded properly). Here are some guidelines to follow…

STEP 1

Choose good tunes – the most important thing you can do is choose top records for the set.

STEP 2

Mix loads of tunes – remember that this is a short demo CD, not a long party. A demo CD that has only a few tunes gets really boring after a few listens.

STEP 3

Be a show off – choose a few tunes that you can mix impressively and throw your best tricks in, so long as they don't come too fast or too quick.

STEP 4

Don't go on too long – one hour is about as much as most people will ever listen to.

STEP 5

Ensure the recording levels are good – most importantly, don't let the volume change! Just as in DJing generally, it's bad news if the listener has to adjust the volume during the set.

TIP

Use the best gear you can get your hands on, clean your records to avoid crackle and get someone to help. If possible, get someone who knows about these things to sit with you for an afternoon and make sure that it all goes well.

EXERCISE

1. Borrow a tape machine and hook it up, as described, for recording your mix. Practise a certain mix of, say, ten records in a set order and then record it. Listen back to the recording of your set and make notes of the best and worst things you hear. If you can bear it, try listening with friends to see what they think. Do remember, however, that you may change your opinion of the tape if you wait a few days – so don't worry too much over today's assessment!

PROBLEM?

If you find that you're making mistakes in your DJing when you record, don't worry about it. You're not playing to an audience of superstar DJs and, most importantly, it's the music you choose that counts.

TEST

QUESTION 1
Why is it important to make a mix tape of yourself?

QUESTION 2
What's the advantage of recording yourself alone at home?

QUESTION 3
What connections do you need from the mixer?

QUESTION 4
Why is using a computer to record your mix the best possible option?

QUESTION 5
What's the most important thing to remember when making a demo CD?

TOP 10 ARTISTS

JUDGE JULES

Judge Jules began DJing as a young teenager and started Radio DJing on the then-pirate radio station, Kiss FM (which went legal in 1990), moving to BBC Radio 1 in October 1997. Jules is said to be the largest crowd-puller on the club circuit and has been titled 'The People's DJ' in the dance music press. Jules also plays regularly in Europe, the US, Brazil, Argentina, Australia, Hong Kong and Singapore (to name but a few). At present Jules is working with Paul Masterson on their 'Hi-Gate' project.

STATISTICS

DATE OF BIRTH
1965

PLACE OF BIRTH
London

INFLUENCES
Rare groove and house

IMPORTANT GIG/VENUE
Shake 'n' Fingerpop and Family Funktion

BIG BREAK
DJing on KISS in the early days

TRUE STORY

Judge Jules got his name because, as a young DJ, he was renowned for providing outrageous legal blags when the police turned up at unauthorised parties hosted by himself and Norman Jay.

IN THE STYLE OF...

LISTEN TO

Kiss In Ibiza '96
Retrospective Of House Vol.1 & Vol.2
Journeys By DJ Vol.2 & Dance Wars
Positiva – Phase One

SUPERSTAR TIP

If you've only just started, a good introduction to mixing is to buy two copies of the same record and try mixing them together. Then slowly learn to adjust the pitch control when mixing different tracks. Ultimately it's all about practice!

Judge Jules' style of music is usually thought of as hard and funky progressive house and disco or, in his own words, 'funky hard house'. On his radio shows, however, he's moved away from 'vocal party house' towards a more banging harder house and trance-y euro sound. He is well known for blending passion with technically-brilliant sets and his eclectic mixing can sometimes surprise even his most dedicated fans.

FATBOY SLIM

Fatboy Slim is the alias of former-Housemartins guitarist Norman Cook. After beginning his post-Housemartins career in the dub band Beats International, he became a dance producer, releasing singles under names such as Freakpower, Pizzaman and Fried Funk Food. Norman, his flatmate Gareth and Skint Records' boss, Damian Harris, decided to give Brighton's like-minded party crowd a permanent venue and called it the Big Beat Boutique. As resident, Norman played records that put a big stupid grin on your face. By the end of 1997 Norman was the undisputed king of big beats and the rest is popstar history.

STATISTICS

DATE OF BIRTH
1967

PLACE OF BIRTH
Brighton

INFLUENCES
Brit rock, Dub and everything in-between

IMPORTANT GIG/VENUE
Playing in Beats International

BIG BREAK
Recording the first Fatboy album

TRUE STORY

Norman was staying at the Chateau Marmont, LA's celebrity hotel, when the title of his follow-up to 'You've Come A Long Way Baby' came to him. 'I was wandering around sweating and shaking, not having been to bed for about two days,' he remembers, 'and I was thinking, you can take the boy out of the gutter but you can't take the gutter out of the boy.'

IN THE STYLE OF...

SUPERSTAR TIP

Play whatever you feel and if anybody tries to tell you what to play, well, thump 'em.

LISTEN TO

'You've Come A Long Way'
'Baby'
'On The Floor At The Boutique'

Fatboy's style is called 'Big Beat' but it's basically just about pure, dumb-ass, stupidly-catchy fun. He somehow manages to blend bits from house, hip hop, rock and soul so naturally that it sounds as if it was originally supposed to sound this way. Most of Fatboy's records tend to take old soul records and put thick, funky break beats over the top of them. In the US, he is credited with having put electronica on the map. His technique is not usually ranked among the best, but his knack for spotting unlikely matches more than makes up for it.

DJ ANGEL

When DJ Angel was growing up, she listened to anything she could find with a good strong vocal, including Rose Royce, Gladys Knight and Shirley Bassey. Her first exposure to club culture was at Nottingham's Rock City where she heard funk, soul and electro. In 1989, she discovered the club Garage and Graeme Park's DJing. Soon afterwards, while working behind the bar at Venus, she debuted on New Year's Eve. Angel was well received, and it led to gigs at Up Your Ronson, the Haçienda and many others. Today, she travels the world as a DJ and spends as much time as possible in the studio.

TRUE STORY

Angel was once (accidentally) booked to play at a trance club and, when she played her funky and mellow house tunes, she cleared the floor!

STATISTICS

DATE OF BIRTH
1970

PLACE OF BIRTH
Nottingham

INFLUENCES
'70s soul and pop

IMPORTANT GIG/VENUE
Swoon in Stafford

BIG BREAK
Venus

IN THE STYLE OF...

LISTEN TO

'Show Me'
'I'm Still Waiting'

Angel plays long, seamless mixes and tends to plays records 'as they were intended to be heard'. She says that being 'trigger happy' on the crossfader 'doesn't usually impress' so she tends to mix more slowly and steadily than most.

SUPERSTAR TIP

The most important thing is to know your records inside out before trying to mix them – once you've heard them 100 times, you'll know them well enough to mix them freely and spontaneously.

DAVE VJ

Dave began by working in record shops and gained musical knowledge that led to a full-time music buyer's position for a music wholesaler. At the same time, he worked as a box boy and technician for the Mastermind sound system, who were known for work at the Notting Hill Carnival. Dave pushed his way on to the decks whenever he could – including London's hip hop hotspot Subterania – and, eventually, established himself as a DJ. After various stints on underground radio he was invited to join Kiss FM, but in 2001 moved to Choice FM where he now hosts the Urban Grid show.

TRUE STORY

VJ stands for Vinyl Junkie. Dave is also a certified lifeguard and swimming instructor.

STATISTICS

DATE OF BIRTH
1970

PLACE OF BIRTH
London

INFLUENCES
Cypress Hill, Public Enemy, classic soul

IMPORTANT GIG/VENUE
Underground radio

BIG BREAK
Job at Kiss FM

IN THE STYLE OF...

LISTEN TO

This Is Hip Hop
Choice FM

Dave VJ is first and foremost a specialist hip hop DJ but he has a style based on hip hop, soul and rap music. His collection of over 30,000 records easily earns him the title 'Vinyl Junkie'. He tends to be quite rough on the decks but never makes mistakes or breaks up.

SUPERSTAR TIP

Radio, production and performance all play a part in the DJ's world. Get involved in as many aspects as you can...

GILLES PETERSON

Gilles has a long history as a DJ starting in South London in the late '70s, where he listened to pirate radio playing jazz, funk and soul. Partly through exposure on his own station he was offered a slot on Radio Invicta. His knowledge and persistence finally set him up to inherit a slot at the Electric Ballroom and then at Nicky Holloway's Special Branch at the Royal Oak. When he landed a show on the then BBC station Radio London, his radio career was assured. His legendary Sunday sessions at Camden's Dingwalls made him a superstar DJ.

TRUE STORY

'One night many years ago, I put on this old 7" by Mickey And The Soul Generation, which was a rare groove record with a mad rock guitar intro and no beat. I started vari-speeding it so it sounded all warped. Chris Bangs got on the microphone and said, 'If that was acid house, this is acid jazz'. That's how acid jazz started – just a joke!'

STATISTICS

DATE OF BIRTH
1965

PLACE OF BIRTH
London

INFLUENCES
DJ Paul Murphy playing rare, killer power jazz

IMPORTANT GIG/VENUE
Electric Ballroom

BIG BREAK
Replacing Paul Murphy

IN THE STYLE OF...

LISTEN TO

The Collection
Gilles Peterson Worldwide

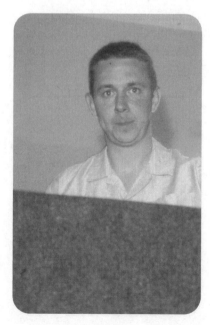

Gilles is truly a one-off. He plays an eclectic mix of jazz, funk, reggae, soul and early electro, and his wider-than-anyone's musical taste and knowledge is his trademark and his style. He is known for inventing 'acid jazz'.

SUPERSTAR TIP

Gilles recommends that young DJs listen to tunes and take lots of notes!

CARL COX

Having grown up listening to his parents' collection of '70s soul, Carl Cox got a pair of decks when he was just 15 and started to practise. From playing friends' parties and learning how to work a crowd, he developed a reputation that gave him his break at the Sunrise rave, just outside London, in 1988. At this gig, he famously hooked up a third deck, and the rest is history… Known ever since as the 'three-deck wizard', Carl DJed at some of the best gigs of the '90s including the opening of Shoom and Brighton's Zap.

STATISTICS

DATE OF BIRTH
1969

PLACE OF BIRTH
London

INFLUENCES
'70s soul

IMPORTANT GIG/VENUE
Sunrise rave

BIG BREAK
Using three decks at Sunrise

TRUE STORY

Carl Cox has been named DJ Of The Year more than five times!

IN THE STYLE OF...

LISTEN TO

Shifting Gear
Club Traxx

Carl Cox is known for banging, funky, tribal, techno music but, well-known as the 'three-deck wizard', his style is more surely based on his brilliant technique. In a typical set, he manages to mix three records together (and sometimes more) for most of the time.

SUPERSTAR TIP

'Let your heart and mind take your music wherever – I went from soul to disco to hip hop and beyond.'

JEREMY HEALY

Jeremy began DJing at parties as far back as 1979, when he already had a habit of playing unconventional 'dance' records such as David Bowie's 'Space Oddity'. At Philip Salon's Planets club, he (with mate Boy George) moved up from coat checker to DJ. Trips to New York's Danceteria and Roxy clubs broadened his musical horizons, and soon he entertained notions of being a pop star. Being around at the birth of UK acid house inspired him, and soon after he wrote and recorded one of the biggest dance anthems ever with his band E-Zee Posse, 'Everything Starts With An E.'

STATISTICS

DATE OF BIRTH
1964

PLACE OF BIRTH
London

INFLUENCES
Anything and everything

IMPORTANT GIG/VENUE
Planet

BIG BREAK
DJing at Planet

TRUE STORY

Jeremy is one of Boy George's oldest friends, and the two of them cut their dance music teeth in New York in the '80s.

IN THE STYLE OF...

LISTEN TO

'House Nation'
'Everything Starts With An E'

Jeremy's style is to have no style. He's known for surprising audiences whenever he plays. He tends to play classic and rare house music tunes, but it's a rare set that doesn't feature something completely bizarre like Led Zeppelin or The Monkees. It's not easy to drop such unusual records into a set, but Jeremy has a style that seems to let him get away with it and always please everybody.

SUPERSTAR TIP

Don't listen to what anyone says – just be true to yourself and play what you like.

TODD TERRY

Although he's best known for his remix of Everything But The Girl's 'Missing', Todd Terry is a lot more than just the DJ who defined New York house in the '80s. His blend of hip hop, house and jungle has made him a US star in the UK for many years. Todd Terry has also made his own music throughout his career and is well respected for his original and varied skills and tastes.

STATISTICS

DATE OF BIRTH
1967

PLACE OF BIRTH
Brooklyn, NY

INFLUENCES
Mainly US dance styles of the '70s and '80s

IMPORTANT GIG/VENUE
New York clubs

BIG BREAK
DJing in NY during the Birth Of It All

TRUE STORY

As a gigging DJ, Todd Terry plays quite varied records. In one recent set, he played Armand Van Helden, Photek and Public Enemy back-to-back.

IN THE STYLE OF...

LISTEN TO

'House Music Movement'
'Ready For A New Day'

SUPERSTAR TIP

'You got to play for the people because they pay your wages...so I try to keep my finger on the pulse.'

He's thought of as a New York house DJ, but Todd Terry made up a whole new style of DJing, back in the day, that's known as 'Todd Terry style'. It uses elements of hip hop, house and jungle, and combines them in a sort of breakbeat way. He calls it 'the melting pot style'.

ALLISTER WHITEHEAD

Allister Whitehead began DJing in his native Nottingham in 1987. He played wherever he could and worked his way up to playing alongside Graeme Park at Coolcat, and eventually headlined his own night at Essence. Though he's mainly a house and garage DJ, Allister's style extends very widely. Since 1996, he's been remixing and making records of his own, as well as hosting a show on Galaxy FM.

STATISTICS

DATE OF BIRTH
1969

PLACE OF BIRTH
Nottingham

INFLUENCES
'70s soul and disco

IMPORTANT GIG/VENUE
Essence

BIG BREAK
Coolcat nights

TRUE STORY

Once during a Cream DJ tour, Allister woke up in Milan, Italy – the worse for wear on the morning after a particularly big gig somewhere in Germany – not actually knowing where he was or how he got there!

IN THE STYLE OF...

LISTEN TO

The House Collection V3
Galaxy Weekend

Allister's style is very straightforward – he plays chunky US-based house and garage tunes, and he leads a crowd wherever he feels like going. His inclusive musical style tends to make any crowd follow him.

SUPERSTAR TIP

'Don't think getting a manager is the answer. Management is the last thing in the jigsaw of a successful career – most big DJs achieve success first and then get a manager.'

SASHA

Sasha (aka Alexander Coe) grew up listening to his dad's Motown records and learning piano. Having learned the basics of DJing in his bedroom, he arrived in Manchester just as the 'Summer of Love' was breaking. He played parties and pubs before finally landing a big break at Shelly's in Stoke. After years of residencies at places like Venus and Renaissance, he now travels the world and keeps residencies at clubs like NY's Twilo.

STATISTICS

DATE OF BIRTH
1973

PLACE OF BIRTH
Wales

INFLUENCES
Motown, movie soundtracks, concept albums

IMPORTANT GIG/VENUE
Renaissance

BIG BREAK
Residency at Shelly's

TRUE STORY

In one of his first gigs, Sasha mixed a piano-led Italian house track while playing a Whitney Houston a cappella track over the top, and this spontaneous creation of a new and exciting record was remembered for years after. He was later pictured on a UK magazine cover with the headline 'Son of God'.

IN THE STYLE OF...

LISTEN TO

**Northern Exposure
The QAT Collection**

Sasha's mixes take elements from across the spectrum of electronic dance (trance, breaks, progressive and deep house). This combination, alongside a wide variety of anthems and sets that take people 'on a journey', keeps dance floors full – and long ago made Sasha a hero.

SUPERSTAR TIP

'DJing is first about being able to read people and then about being able to tap into that human experience and take it on a journey.'

STYLES OF MUSIC

As Scratch has said quite a few times already, it's the music that counts more than anything else! No matter how good your skills get, you'll never be more popular than the music you play.

The most popular DJs, even if they are brilliant and quick and tricky, are known for the particular style of music that they play. In the same way, you will have to choose a style or genre to specialise in. There are hundreds of genres and sub-genres and sub-sub-genres of dance music in the world, and you should definitely try to listen to as many of them as you possibly can. Always do at least a bit of style-combining to give your set something fresh and unique, but mainly you'll have to tie yourself to one (or possibly two) styles.

The most important thing to remember is that, whatever you choose, you have to really love it. Don't try choosing something just because its popular or rare or it's likely to get you gigs. If you don't love what you play, then you're unlikely to ever get any good at it – and besides, you'll come to hate DJing after awhile if you do!

Of the many, many styles out there, here are a few:

ACID
Acid house is often seen as the mother of all of today's dance music. Usually the defining element is the presence of that caustic, metallic, 'acidic' noise that comes from the old Roland TR303, but it's not strictly necessary. Acid music features big breakdowns and simple beats.

AMBIENT
This is a loose term but it usually indicates that music is sparse or that it at least features long, empty sections. Using movie soundtracks and avant-garde pop records, Sasha helped turn this genre into a worldwide movement. Such wide spaces in the music make it easy to mix.

BIG BEAT & BREAKBEAT
Usually with a house or garage-style tempo, the beats and samples are actually closer to hip hop. Fatboy Slim brought this genre to the mainstream.

DEEP HOUSE
As another foundation stone of dance music, deep house originated in Chicago and is closely related to house and acid, though it uses vocals and instruments in soulful and funky features.

DISCO
Disco is less a genre than an element and an inspiration. Many modern styles incorporate disco beats, samples and songs. The original disco records from the '70s tend to sound quite thin and tinny against the huge bass sounds of today.

DRUM'N'BASS
As a follow-on from jungle, D'n'B is fast and furious. The beats are frenetic and the song structures are as free as the wind, so be careful when mixing and don't let your attention stray from the record at all.

HARD HOUSE
Combining the wild and nasty big rave synth sounds of the early '90s with banging techno beats, hard house generally appeals to younger audiences that have the energy to keep up and the ability to put up with hoover noises.

HOUSE (AND US GARAGE)
House is the most basic and effective music for a young DJ to mix because the beats are straightforward and the songs are structured in uniformly square and easily predictable chunks of round numbers of bars. US house and garage was pioneered by Todd Terry in New York in the '80s. If you lose your place in a house record, you can always just wait for it to come round again – which it always does in another 8 or 16 bars. Also, the best a cappella mixes tend to be at the end of old house records.

R'N'B

Actually, this is just the word for soul music, though it tends to feature hip-hop beats, funky rhythms and even rap. This genre can be harder to mix because it requires good awareness and judgment of vocals, melody and musical structure. Mind you, you get to listen to seriously soulful tunes and stonking vocals.

RAGGA

Reggae fans can easily get hooked on this if they dig the rapped vocals called 'toasting'. The tempos tend to vary widely, which can make it difficult to mix unless you carefully choose your set and stick to it.

RAP

The trouble with rap records for DJs is that there are virtually no rules – anything goes! The tunes tend to stop randomly, change tempo in the middle and generally ambush the DJ. Solution: know your records like the back of your, erm, hand.

TECHNO

The combination of electro-pop and house yielded the most minimal of four-to-the-floor genres. Classic techno features wildly modern sci-fi sounds and aggressive machine noises. Done well, this can be a joy to mix. Done badly, it can give everyone within earshot a migraine.

TRANCE & PROGRESSIVE

Born out of European early '90s psychedelia, Trance usually features relentless pulsing synth sequences designed to induce hypnosis. It's easy and fun to mix and pretty much everyone will enjoy it, at least for a little while.

UK GARAGE

Soulful vocals on top of rough drum'n'bass-style bass lines with swinging beats makes for an enticing choice to a young DJ. It's especially great for mixing using the basic techniques and tricks. Do, however, be careful of song structures, which tend to be irregular – often for the sake of it.

WHERE TO GO FROM HERE

Whatever style you choose, the key to success is to listen. Buy, beg, steal or borrow as many records of the genre that you possibly can and set aside a lot of time to go through them. Even the records that you don't fancy will likely teach you something (even if it's just that you don't fancy them!) When you come across a record that you like and that you think you might mix, listen to it a few times – and then some more. If special features or sections present themselves as ideas for mixing in a set, write them down and keep a long list. Only after you've heard many, many tunes – many, many times – should you turn to the list to start chopping and combining ingredients for your rhythmic stew.

The best DJ is the one who knows his tunes like the back of his hand.

So now you know the score – put the needle on the record and spin, spin, spin... You've come a long way in a short time, but now you need to get serious. This book has given you the tips and the moves, and you've done well to get through them all. Unfortunately, as in life, it's never over coz you can always get better. Even Scratch is still improving! Really! Everyday I find some scratch or some twist that I didn't know before and I think: 'There's a new one on me!' So I know, from first-hand knowledge, that you can't know everything and you can't get too good. All you can do is keep practising to keep getting better.

Don't forget that you can always go back and repeat chapters from this book when you think you need help in a certain area. I often repeat the exercises from the middle chapters just to stay in shape.

Well, it's been real jammin' with ya, and I hope I see you in clubland someday – maybe even as a superstar DJ! You never know! And, after all, it happened to me! JUST KEEP ON PRACTISING!

CD CONTENTS

1. BB MILES
'TIBET'
138 BPM

This tune has a dangerous intro because the first sound you hear is not, in fact, a 'beat one' but rather a note that occurs between beats one and two (if you were to cue it from the first sound you would find that it runs out of sync.) To avoid problems with tunes that you suspect start on a different beat, always cue them from later into the tune, such as from the first bass drum. There is also a big breakdown at about 1:00. Though the tempo is fast, this tune is a relentless four-on-the-floor so is easy to mix.

2. TOMMY WASHINGTON
'HEAVEN'
132 BPM

A very long intro, with no bass drum, precedes the first drum entry. When the bass drum finally does enter, be careful because it has gaps for a few bars before finally becoming steady. Also, this one has some vocals and quite a bit of music instrumentation in the middle, so be sure to mix out early on, unless your other tune matches it well. You may notice that the vocals are featured in a 'gated' effect sound.

3. BIG AL
'AL'S THEME'
128 BPM

The intro on this one features a big synth-sound riff, but because of its sampley nature, you may find that it works with almost anything else. Beware of the cymbal crashes that play on beats that are not the beginning of a phrase. There is a big breakdown at 3:40 that is a useful in-point but be careful of the fake ending at 6:00.

4. BAM BAM
'TAKE ME AWAY'
126 BPM

This has a huge bass sound at the intro that may work well over some other tune's drums. In the body of the tune there is a lot of instrumentation, vocals and even a saxophone riff, so be sure to check what works with it musically before beat-mixing it. There is quite a sudden ending as well, so be sure to mix out well before it.

5. BB MILES
'EVERYDAY'
138 BPM

This tune is straight up: very easy beat and useful breakdowns. There's also only one chord in the music so it tends to work well over almost anything. Do be careful of too many notes, though, as the sequences and drum patterns are very busy.

6. ALTO YORK
'REAL LOVE'
127 BPM

The percussion front is long (and useful for scratching) and leads to a big bass line and vocal sample before finally dropping into a full lead vocal. Note the vocal has 'flanger' effect. The sax line may be too musical for beat mixing but there's a good drum and percussion outro from 4:45 and a breakdown to bass only at 5:20 with just bass drum and sample sequences to mix out on. You'd find it easy to mix this one all the way out.

7 COBANA
'COCA CABANA'
130 BPM

The soft sequence sounds at the intro might be difficult to mix but a good percussion build follows that is very simple and useful. Note the whole mix in a 'phasing' effect at 3:30 and 5:00 and be careful of the sudden ending.

8. B M EX
'MACHIQUE'
125 BPM

This one has a trance front that works over anything as a sort of sci-fi sound effect. It's very ambient and empty with high-pitched percussion sounds entering after about 30 seconds. The bass drum enters at about 1:00 and this would be an easy in-point. The music and vocal don't hit until nearly 2:00 so this is a useful and easy intro for mixing. Note the 're-intro' at 3:15, which could be used against the first, proper intro in a mix or, with two copies, as a variation on phasing.

9 WHITE HOUSE
'MOUNTAIN' (INSTRUMENTAL)
128 BPM

While this version is meant to be mixed under the next a cappella version, it is also a good one to mix alone because the intro is a good, solid and lengthy house beat. There's no music until well after 1:00, but when it comes, it's huge.

10. WHITE HOUSE 'MOUNTAIN' (A CAPPELLA) 128 BPM

This is the a cappella (vocals only) that fits squarely on top of the instrumental. Note that the very first sound falls, in fact, halfway between beats one and two, so try to drop it in right after you hear the second kick drum in the instrumental.

NOTES

NOTES

NOTES

GLOSSARY

A CAPPELLA
A song or mix that contains only vocals – with no drums, melody or other instruments accompanying.

AGENT
A person who organises a DJ's bookings, and usually takes about 10 per cent of the fee.

AMPLIFIER, AMP
A piece of equipment that increases the signal from the mixer so that a pair (or pairs) of speakers can be powered. Some speakers are 'self-powered', with built-in amplifiers, but the majority require a separate amp to operate.

ANALOGUE
Old-style equipment. The opposite of digital.

ANTI-SKATING
A feature found on professional turntables that prevents the needle from skipping across the record.

AUX (OR LINE IN)
Abbreviation for 'auxiliary', meaning secondary or supplementary. In the case of DJ equipment, such as a mixer or amplifier, the 'aux' input socket allows a secondary piece of equipment to be plugged in (eg a CD player). If you would like to record yourself mixing, your mixer should connect to the AUX socket on your hi-fi or stereo.

BAR
A collection of beats. Usually there are four beats per bar.

BATTLE
A hip hop or drum'n'bass DJ competition in which DJs compete against each other in short sets showcasing their skills and track selection.

BATTLE-STYLE
A way of orienting the turntables so that the tone arm sides of the decks are furthest away from the DJ, as opposed to the usual layout where the tone arm is to the right of the DJ. This method prevents the DJ's arms from brushing the tone arm and disrupting their set in the heat of a battle.

BEAT
A single pulse (or unit of rhythmical noise) in music. It can be made up of several notes or fractions of a note. The most common beats come four per bar (a '4/4' time signature).

BEAT COUNTER
An electronic device that counts the beats per minute (bpm) of a track.

BEATMATCHING
The art of synchronising two separate records in time, which have different speeds or tempos.

BEAT JUGGLING
This skill is done by using two records and manipulating the arrangement of the elements (drum sounds, headnotes, vocals etc) from both to create a new-sounding track. For example, in a very simple beat juggle one or

more bars of record A are played, then the DJ quickly flips the crossfader to the beatmatched record B for one or more bars, then back to A and so on.

BIAS
When the crossfader or cue mix is output at a higher volume on one channel it is said to be 'biased' to that channel. If the crossfader is more to the right hand side, it is more biased to the right channel than it is to the left.

BELT DRIVE
One of the major differences between turntables is whether they are belt or direct drive. Belt drive turntables have their platter driven by a thick 'rubber band' compared to the more expensive type of turntable (direct drive) which is driven by a motor directly.

BLENDING
When a DJ mixes two tracks during the ambient or beatless part of one or both tracks, they are blending the two tracks, as opposed to beatmatching or any other method of mixing.

BODY
The main part of a track's tune – between the intro and the breakdown.

BPM
Short for beats per minute. The bpm indicates the speed of an individual track. An easy way to count the bpm of a track is to

count the number of beats occurring in 60 seconds.

BREAK

The part of a track where the song generally fades down to an ambient, or beatless, section or the main rhythmic drums are reduced or left standing by the removal of the melody of the track. These can be seen on the vinyl as smoother areas.

BREAKBEAT

This genre is basically a beat with a 'break' or gap in the continuity of the snare drums.

BREAKDOWN

Part of a track after the intro and before the outro where the beat slows or stops, creating tension before the next section.

BREAKS

Or Breakbeat. A genre of music that incorporates a breakbeat rhythm and a bpm of around 120–40.

BUILD, BUILD UP

The areas after the breaks in a record where the track builds in melodic tension, before hitting the main body of the tune.

CARTRIDGE

The main part of the needle, attached to the end of the tone arm, where vibrations from the stylus are converted into electrical impulses.

CENTRE SPINDLE

Or spindle. This is the blunt spike that points up in the middle of the platter. To play a record you place record on over the spindle. The spindle can be manipulated with the fingers to make fine adjustments to the speed of a record when beatmatching.

CHANNEL

One vertical section on a mixer, representing one turntable's output into the system.

CHANNEL FADER

The channel faders allow you to control the individual volume of each channel by the use of a slider or knob.

CHANNEL SELECTOR

This allows you to choose between different input sources, that you have plugged into the back of your mixer.

COUNTER WEIGHT

The counter weight is situated towards the back of the tone arm and is responsible for the amount of pressure (or weight) the needle exerts on the record. If your needle is skipping it can help to increase the counterweight on it, but applying too much pressure can damage the record.

CROSSFADER

Also fader, x-fader or Hamster switch. The crossfader is a main component of the mixer, allowing you to fade between individual channels or play two channels simultaneously.

CUEING

The act of finding the exact spot within the next record you intend to play, usually done in the headphones so that the audience can't hear it.

CUE BURN

The act of cueing a record up repeatedly in one spot, as in hip hop DJing and scratching, can wear the groove in the record at that point down. This results in cue burn, which can cause the record to skip.

CUE LEVEL

The cue level controls the volume of sound playing through the headphones. Normally found on the mixer.

CUEING LEVER

This lever is used to gently lower the needle on to the vinyl without scratching it – but this is never used by the cooler DJs.

CUE MIX

The cue mix allows you to hear what is being played on each channel through the headphones. You can also listen to both channels simultaneously and some mixers allow you to pan between the cue mix and what is currently being heard through the main speakers.

DB

A measurement of volume. 'dB' stands for decibel, which is the official unit used to measure the level of sound.

DIGITAL
A kind of equipment in which the data needed to run it is stored as a string of numbers as 1's and 0's. The opposite of analogue.

DIRECT DRIVE
One of the major differences between turntables is whether they are belt or direct drive. Direct drive turntables have their platter driven directly by a motor, compared to the less expensive type of turntable (belt drive) that have their platter driven by a thick rubber band.

DOWNTEMPO
Also down tempo, down beat.

DRUM AND BASS
Also d'n'b; drum'n'bass. This genre could be described as speeded-up breakbeats with a slower bass line. The speed of the drums varies from 140–70 bpm; the bass line is – sometimes – half of the speed of the drum. The drums have the breakbeat 1 2 3 4, which means that the 2 and 4 are snare or kick drum on the floor, while the 1, sometimes, and the 3, hardly always, are drums (ie off the measure).

EQ
Two or three knobs on a mixer used to adjust the levels of bass, (maybe mid range) and treble. There is often a set of dials for each individual channel on the mixer.

EXIT (OR OUTRO)
Part of a track's structure the exit is the last bars where several elements are usually dropped out to leave a simpler version of the track to mix out of.

FADER
A slider, usually the channel fader, but it could refer to the Master Output fade or the crossfader.

FILTER
Also effects. An effect with which a tune can be modified without altering the tempo. Many mixers come with effects filters, such as flange, reverb, echo, etc, which can be used on one or more channels to change the sound of the track. Additional effects devices can also be routed through your mixer to add filter to tunes while you play.

FLIGHT CASE
A record carrying case designed to protect your vinyl from the effects of heat and rough handling during transit.

GAIN
How much an electronic circuit amplifies a signal is called its 'gain'. Sometimes used for 'volume'.

GENRE
A single category (or kind) of music, marked by a distinctive style, form or content.

GROUND, GROUNDING
The wire hanging from the back of a deck that needs to be connected to the grounding screw on the back of a mixer to prevent the 'hum' of feedback.

HAMSTER SWITCH
The crossfader. Or, sometimes, a switch on some mixers that reverses the turntable so that the right channel swaps with the left. It is used in scratching to create effects.

HEADPHONES
Placed on your head so you can hear an incoming track while mixing, headphones are an essential part of DJing.

HEADSHELL
The headshell joins directly on to the tone arm, providing a protective housing unit for the cartridge to attach to.

HI-FI
Short for high fidelity.

HOUSE
1. A genre of music with four bass drums per bar beat: 1 2 3 4 at about 120 bpm – about the speed of the heart of the dancer. On the 2 and 4, there is a snare drum or hand clap; in between 1 2 3 4 of the bass drum, are hi hats.
2. The word house also refers to the main club or event space, as opposed to the DJ booth.

INPUT SELECTOR
The input selector is found on the mixer alongside the channel fader. The input selector enables you to switch from different input

sources – another turntable or CD player for example. This means that a mixer with two channels can make use of more than just two inputs.

INTRO
The beginning of a track before the main theme is introduced.

JUNGLE
The Jungle was the name of a notorious area in the city of Kingston, Jamaica, where reggae and dancehall beats evolved into what we now know as a form of drum'n'bass called jungle.

JUNGLIST
A jungle DJ or someone who enjoys jungle drum'n'bass.

KILL SWITCH
The kill switch will instantly drop one channel's output, or the bass, mid range or treble of a channel, out of the mix which is useful for effects where the DJ drops one track out for a bar, or a beat or more. Kill switches accomplish this more cleanly than trying to slide the crossfader over quickly or slide the channel fader down fast.

LABEL
1. A record label – part of a (larger) record company that usually has many labels under its roof.
2. The paper sticker in the middle of a record on which the artist's name, title and other information about the track are printed.

LEVELS
The relative levels of highs, mids and bass output through the channels of a mixer when DJing. If you're asked by a sound engineer, the owner of the sound system or another interested party to 'check your levels', you should take that as a subtle hint that you are playing with too much treble, bass, etc, and should adjust the equalisers to improve the sound of your set.

LINE OR AUX
Input socket on DJ equipment (mixers etc) and high quality audio equipment allowing line devices such as CD players to be connected.

LIVE
Playing live is producing music spontaneously with the use of synths, drum machines, etc, while DJing. (When used with reference to a turntable, if a deck is live it is the one currently playing out through the house speakers.)

LOOP
Part of a track's structure, a loop is usually made of 4–8 bars.

MASTER VOLUME
The slider or knob that controls the overall volume that will be pumped out through the speakers.

MINIDISC
A small-format digital playback (and often recording) machine. Very useful as a recording machine at gigs (so you can check your performance later at home).

MIX
1. A mix is when two songs are mixed together using beatmatching, beat juggling or a simple fade across the breaks in two tracks. It can be as long or short as the DJ likes. DJs often try to make their mixes as individual and as interesting as possible.
2. To mix is the act of creating a mix.

MIXER
One of the main pieces of equipment needed to DJ. The mixer allows you to combine two separate sound sources and play them as one.

NEEDLE
Another term for a stylus.

NUMARK®
Manufacturer of DJ equipment such as mixers and turntables.

OUTPUT DISPLAY
The LED display that shows which channel the crossfader has more bias towards, and/or the level of the master volume.

OUTRO
Also Exit. Part of a track's structure, the outro is the last set of bars where several elements are usually dropped out to leave a simpler version of the track to mix out of.

PANASONIC®

Panasonic® is one of the worlds leading manufacturers of audio equipment and makes the legendary Technics® turntables, which are the industry standard.

PICK UP TIME

The time taken for the platter to get up to the desired speed from stopped. This will largely depend on whether you are using belt or direct drive turntables (direct drive being the fastest and best).

PITCH

1. The relative position of a musical tone within the musical range ('high' or 'low')
2. The percentage speed at which a track is playing on a turntable. The pitch can be altered using the pitch control and is referred to as plus 4 or minus 6, etc.

PITCH BEND

On CD mixers the pitch bend (like a pitch control) allows the pitch of the track you are playing to be sped up or slowed down.

PITCH CONTROL

On turntables, the pitch control is a slider on the right-hand side allowing you to change the speed that the record is played. Typically the pitch can be altered +/- 8%

PLATTER

1. The platter is the circular metal plate that the motor drives.
2. A platter is also a term used for a record.

PROMO

A record that has not been officially released by a record label. It is commonly referred to as a white label and is generally given to well known DJs to play before the tune is released in order to generate hype.

PUSHING OFF

When a DJ pushes the record off so that the beats will match with those on another deck immediately, while the channel volume is up.

QUARTZ LOCK

A function found on professional turntables that allows the speed of the platter to remain constant (locked)

RPM

RPM stands for revolutions per minute (the amount of times the record revolves in any given minute). There are two distinct types of records: 33rpm and 45rpm – though a third type (78rpm) is sometimes seen.

RPM ADAPTER

Some vinyl, in particular those that are made to be played at 45 rpm, have a large hole cut out of the centre. (The reason for this extends back to the old days when vinyl was played in juke boxes). In order for you to play these records on your turntables the adapter is placed on the centre spindle to increase the size.

SAMPLE

A short sound. (Or an extracted phrase from another source, eg another record, CD or a sound you have burnt to CD, which is added to a live or pre-recorded mix to create a new sound.)

SAMPLER

A sort of synth or keyboard or machine used to play pre-programmed samples by the pressing of buttons or keys.

SCRATCHING

The sound produced when the vinyl is run back and forth under the needle.

SENNHEISER®

Sennheiser® is one of the leading manufacturers of audio equipment. Their range of headphones is favoured by many of the worlds' leading DJs.

SEAMLESS

This is used to describe the quality of a DJ's mixing. If done perfectly with interruptions it is said to be seamless.

SELECTOR

Also Selecta, Record Selector. A slang term for a DJ.

SKIPPING

When the tone arm is not correctly adjusted with enough pressure from the counter weight, the needle may slide (or 'skip') over the grooves in a record. The movement of people on the dance floor is often enough to create a skip.

SLIPMATS

Slipmats are the circular pieces of felt placed between the platter and the record.

SPINBACK

A spinback, or performing a spinback (also known as a backspin) is when the DJ stops a record with their hand and rewinds it quickly.

STYLUS

Commonly referred to as the needle, the stylus is in fact the tiny piece of metal that reads the grooves of the record.

TARGET LIGHT

The target light is that little pop-up light that shines across your vinyl allowing you to tell in the dark how far into the record you have played, and where all the breakdowns are.

TECHNO

A genre of music featuring mechanical beats and found sounds that range from apocalyptic sirens to sampled TV and movie dialogue. It was developed in Detroit in the early '80s and has a tempo of around 126–30 bpm.

TEMPO

The speed of a track measured in bpms (beats per minute)

THEME

In the structure of a track, themes are usually 4 to 32 bars. They make up the main body of the tune, carry the melody and are the part you usually hum when remembering a tune.

TINNITUS

The affliction that damages your ears due to exposure to high decibels of sound over extended periods.

TONE ARM

The tone arm is the long metal arm that is attached at the top right hand side of the turntable. The stylus and cartridge are attached to the end of this. Usually S-shaped, although straight tone arms are becoming ever more popular as they are supposed to prevent skipping.

TRANSFORM, TO

The use of a crossfader or on/off switch to produce a very fast stuttering sound of the input source (usually used in scratching).

VESTAX®

One of the leading manufacturers of DJ equipment.

VINYL

1. What records are made of.
2. Also another name for records themselves.

VOCAL

Vocals are the singing or spoken voice part of a track.

WARPING

If you leave your precious vinyls out in the sun or pack them too tightly in your crate, or stack them unevenly, they can warp, or bend – rendering them useless. You can attempt to fix your warped records by putting them on the turntable and using a hairdryer on a low setting to try and melt it back into shape.

WAX

Another name for records.

WHEELS OF STEEL

A commonly used name for turntables.

WHITE LABEL

This is a record that has no information on the label. Generally a promo, it's usually given to well-known DJs to play before the tune is released in order to generate hype.

X-FADER

Another name used for the crossfader. It's the main component of the mixer allowing you to fade between individual channels or play two channels simultaneously.

ANSWERS TO TEST QUESTIONS

LESSON 1
1. Turntable, mixer, cartridge, slipmat, headphones, amp and speakers.
2. The screw at the back of the mixer.
3. Tone arm weighting.

LESSON 2
1. A note is played by an instrument or sung by a singer, while a beat is just a pulse in any song (that might be played or might be silent).
2. In dance music, there are always four beats in a bar.
3. The second and fourth beats of every bar, marked by the snare drum.

LESSON 3
1. It allows you to listen only to that channel in the headphones, so that the audience doesn't hear you cueing up and so you don't hear the other record that is playing over the speakers.
2. It switches (or 'fades') from one channel to the other and, while it's in the middle you can hear both channels at the same time in the speakers.
3. The spot on a record from where you're going to bring it into the mix – and from where the audience will first hear it.

LESSON 4
1. Speed refers to the rate the turntable spins at (like 33rpm, 45rpm, or plus 3% on the vari-speed), while tempo refers to the rate the beat of the song runs at (like 125 bpm or 135 bpm).
2. A group of bars – usually

4, 8 or 16.
3. Beat mixing is when a DJ plays two records at the same time, and adjusts the speed of one of them until that they run in sync.
4. By brushing your fingers along the side of the record to slow it down a bit or by gently squeezing the centre spindle.

LESSON 5
1. Up to +8% (and it also can slow it down by up to –8 %).
2. It might make the record sound unnaturally fast or slow – like Mickey Mouse or Darth Vader.
3. If the overall mix gets louder on a drop mix or beat mix, the audience will need the volume to then stay that loud and it is impossible to make every new record louder than the one before – or you'll soon blow up the system!
4. By moving the second channel fader up as you move the first one down during a changeover to a new record. (But remember that only the top couple of centimetres will make any difference, because you can't really hear much of a channel when the fader is at halfway or below!)
5. Vocals and bass lines.

LESSON 6
1. It controls whether the channel will listen to its 'phono' input or its 'line' input on the back of the mixer.
2. The fast on/off sound that comes from toggling the

line/phono switch quickly and rhythmically.
3. When you switch over to another (beatmatched) record for just a couple of beats to pick up the end of a phrase (a fill).
4. A clever way to mix out of a record by (suddenly) spinning that record sharply backwards with your fingers, and then quickly crossfading to a new tune on the beat.

LESSON 7
1. The sound effect that results from two copies of the same record being mixed together so closely that they almost sound as one.
2. Mixing two records together exactly half a beat apart and then using the crossfader to switch between them quickly.
3. A mix of a tune on a record that has only the vocals, with no instruments or drums at all.

LESSON 8
1. The slipmat must be very slippy (or you can't scratch at all!).
2. When you move the record back and forth quickly under the needle (usually to the beat of another record).
3. Percussion and drum sounds (though often an a cappella vocal is equally brilliant).
4. A freaked-out scratch where the music shimmers. (OK, I know that's a naughty and unfair answer, but, hey, it's funny!)

LESSON 9

1. They weigh a lot less, the machines are very simple to use and you can store cue points for quick cueing and looping.
2. It stops the CD a short time before the tune – when you need to be able to control and adjust the amount of space before the song that you want each time.
3. Repeating a phrase or section of a tune so perfectly and smoothly that it sounds as if the tune itself actually was supposed to go that way originally.
4. A computer music file.
5. They are 'compressed' so they're much smaller and take up a lot less memory than other kinds of computer music files (like .wav).

LESSON 10

1. To hear yourself mixing so you can identify your good and bad points for improving your skills.
2. You can do as many takes as you need to get it right.
3. Just connect the 'master outputs' of the club's mixer to the inputs of your recording machine.
4. Because you can seamlessly edit together the best bits of several mixes – thereby making you sound even better than you actually are!
5. Choose good tunes!